What's Your Style?

STREETWEAR
FASHION

STEPHANIE WATSON

Lerner Publications Company
Minneapolis

Lerner Publications Company
A division of Lerner Publishing Group, Inc.
241 First Avenue North
Minneapolis, MN 55401 U.S.A.

For reading levels and more information, look up this title at www.lernerbooks.com.

Credits: Amy Fitzgerald and Sara E. Hoffmann (editorial), Emily Harris (design), Giliane Mansfeldt (photos), Heidi Hogg (production)

Main body text set in Adrianna Light 12/14.
Typeface provided by Chank.

Library of Congress Cataloging-in-Publication Data

Watson, Stephanie, 1969–
     Streetwear fashion / by Stephanie Watson.
         pages   cm. — (What's your style?)
     Includes index.
     ISBN 978-1-4677-1471-6 (lib. bdg : alk. paper)
     ISBN 978-1-4677-2530-9 (eBook)
     1. Fashion—United States—Juvenile literature. 2. Clothing and dress—
United States—Juvenile literature. I. Title.
TT507.W383 2014
746.9'2—dc23   2013017734

Manufactured in the United States of America
1 – PC – 12/31/13

What's Your Style?

CONTENTS

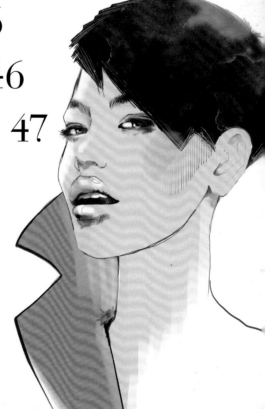

IS STREETWEAR for You?

Do you love the casual urban look? Then maybe streetwear fashion is your thing. Take this quiz to find out if streetwear style suits you.

1. What vibe do you try to create with the outfits you wear?
   a. wild and flashy
   b. classic and perfectly put together
   c. lazy and sloppy
   d. relaxed but creative

2. When it comes to T-shirts, you prefer
   a. plain black
   b. sparkly or sequined—or both!
   c. none! Only polos and oxfords will do!
   d. colorful, with a unique design or logo

3. Before you leave home, you always put on your
   a. creeper shoes
   b. fedora
   c. stretchy headband
   d. hoodie

4. Which singer has a fashion sense you love?
   a. Beyoncé
   b. Katy Perry
   c. Taylor Swift
   d. Gwen Stefani

5. If you had an unlimited allowance to spend on clothes, you'd put it toward a brand-new
   a. pair of diamond studs
   b. party dress
   c. designer hat
   d. varsity jacket

6. Where do you get your clothes?
   a. a department store
   b. a boutique
   c. at home—you make them yourself!
   d. all of the above

If you answered mostly *d*'s, you're a **streetwear** star! This style is all about being unique—a fun, free rebel.

Unlike most fashions, streetwear came from the street to the fashion runways—not the other way around. It's laid-back and stylish at the same time. And it's flexible. You can make your own designs, or you can put your own spin on clothes you buy. Streetwear shows your personal style—not some designer's!

Who's Got
THE LOOK?

Streetwear started with surfers on the beaches of California. Then skaters picked up on it. Eventually streetwear crossed the country to the East Coast. Hip-hop artists put their own urban spin on it. More recently, streetwear has caught on in Japan, where young trendsetters have taken the look in daring and quirky new directions.

If you're looking for some fashion inspiration, turn to your favorite celebs for style ideas. Here's how the stars show off their streetwear style.

GWEN STEFANI

As a singer and fashion designer, Gwen Stefani is no stranger to the spotlight—but she also knows her way around the street. She's been on board with streetwear since her career started in the '80s, and you can still spot her making her mark with

- bold colors, from red jeans to mustard-colored shoes (but not together!);

- bright red lipstick and simple but striking hairstyles; and

- endlessly inventive variations on staple items such as pants and shorts—ranging from baggy to skintight, and from solid colors to crazy prints.

Gwen likes distinctive patterns that catch the eye but don't go overboard.

Check out these other street-smart celebs!

PINK

DEMI LOVATO

SHAUN WHITE

JAY-Z

This hip-hop mogul can afford any style he wants. But Jay-Z is a big fan of streetwear. He was one of the first rappers to show his love for this style. These days, he still wears

- T-shirts, jeans, and snapback hats when he's not in the mood for a high-fashion suit;

- hoodies and logo sweatshirts when the temperature drops; and

- flashy jewelry, from watches to pendants.

Jay-Z rocks snapback hats.

KYLIE JENNER

As a teen model and a member of reality television royalty—best known for her appearances on her family's hit show, *Keeping Up with the Kardashians*—Kylie Jenner knows how to make an impression. And she often rocks the fashion boat by incorporating elements of streetwear into her personal style. You might see Kylie sporting

- distinctive logo T-shirts;

- chunky gold jewelry;

- hoodies and beanies on lazy hair days;

- colorful dresses with eye-catching patterns; and

- killer boots and heels with daring designs.

Kylie (left) often wears her hair in a bun and accents her low-key makeup with dark eyeliner.

RIHANNA

This superstar and style icon is so into streetwear that she's got her own clothing line. When she goes out, she likes to mix styles, combining runway fashion with a more down-to-earth look. For example, she might wear a designer dress with high-top sneakers and a snapback hat. "I love a high-end bag or jacket with a simple dress," she says. Her favorite streetwear looks include

- sports jerseys and big varsity jackets over logo T-shirts;

- oversized work boots and high-top sneakers;

- snapback hats worn backward; and

- plenty of gold bling.

How Do I GET THE LOOK?

The streetwear look is easy to get. It's all around you! A lot of the clothes that you already own are probably in line with streetwear style. You just need to learn how to combine and personalize them to get the right look.

The building blocks of streetwear—such as T-shirts, shorts, and sneakers—couldn't be more basic. The only secret ingredient is your creativity!

The Birth of **Streetwear**

Streetwear was born in the early 1980s. Shawn Stussy—a surfer in Laguna Beach, California—started selling plain T-shirts with his signature printed on them. Other surfers loved his designs. Within a few years, Shawn's shirts, shorts, and hats were an international hit. Aside from the unique logo, all the clothes were simple. "I just make basic clothes that a 10-year-old can wear and my dad can wear," Shawn explained.

Skateboarder Tony Hawk is all about the casual streetwear look.

Surfer Cool

It all started with surfer Shawn Stussy. The basics of his look were long shorts, logo T-shirts, and slip-on sneakers. He and his friends didn't "put much money into clothes. We don't want to look like we're trying too hard, you know," as Shawn put it. Decades later, streetwear is still low-maintenance and easy to build from scratch.

The hip-hop group Run-DMC embraced streetwear in the 1980s.

Hip-Hop Chic

In the 1980s and the 1990s, hip-hop artists added their style to streetwear. Elements of this look—hoodies, oversized jeans, snapback hats, and big sneakers with fat laces—have been popular ever since.

Round-the-World
Radical

Since the early 2000s, Japanese teens have been on the cutting edge of the global streetwear scene. Their elaborate homemade costumes are colorful, layered, and theatrical. Outfits often represent characters from books or legend. They can also echo bygone times—from the European Middle Ages to the nineteenth-century American West. If you're looking to express your wild side, take your cue from these imaginative trailblazers!

Teens show off their streetwear looks on Takeshita Street, a famous pedestrian shopping street and trendy fashion district in Tokyo, Japan.

BRAND-OLD

Most fashion trends are all about buying the latest styles. Not streetwear. The older the clothes, the more popular they are. When streetwear first kicked off, many of the clothes were made in small batches. Today, they're very collectible. The original streetwear clothes are called vintage. Some are worth a lot of money.

MAKE YOUR OWN STREETWEAR BRAND

Streetwear opens fashion up to everyone. It's all about "getting your name out there and getting up in this world," said Erik Marino, cofounder of the Rocksmith brand. Many streetwear designers started their brands while they were still in high school. You can do that too! All you need is some fabric paint and T-shirts. Then you can create a look that expresses your own personal style.

So now you've got the big picture. What about the nuts and bolts? When it comes to streetwear, girls' and boys' styles blur. You can wear a dress or go with a hoodie and a baseball cap. It's totally up to you! But to style yourself in streetwear, you do need to have a few basic pieces in your wardrobe.

T-SHIRTS

The T-shirt is one of the most important pieces in the streetwear look. "T-shirts are viral; you see them as you walk around," says Jeff Ng, founder of the clothing line Staple. "For our generation . . . [making a statement on] t-shirts and cotton is more effective than paper and canvas, where you have to go to a gallery space or museum to see it." Don't settle for just any old T-shirt, though. A cool logo is a must. That logo could be the lyrics to a song. It could be a picture of a pop star or model. Or it could be a design you draw yourself. Your T-shirts can be oversized, or you can go for a more fitted look. If sleeves are a turn-off in summertime, a logo tank top is another option.

HOODIES

If the weather outside is chilly, you can throw a hooded sweatshirt over your T-shirt. Hoodies come in all colors and designs—even camouflage. You can wear the hood up or down. It all depends on your mood—and how cold it is outside.

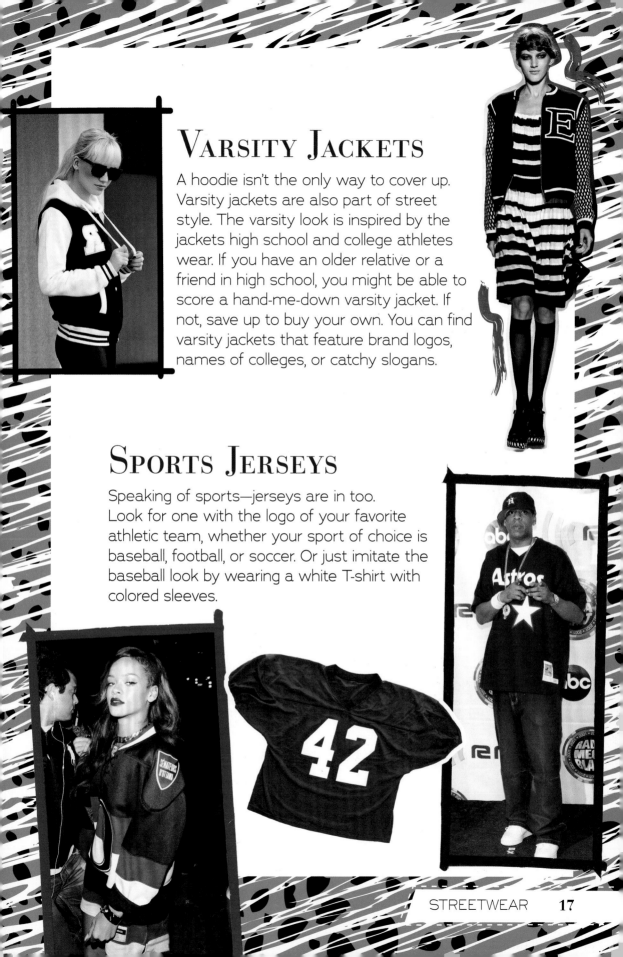

VARSITY JACKETS

A hoodie isn't the only way to cover up. Varsity jackets are also part of street style. The varsity look is inspired by the jackets high school and college athletes wear. If you have an older relative or a friend in high school, you might be able to score a hand-me-down varsity jacket. If not, save up to buy your own. You can find varsity jackets that feature brand logos, names of colleges, or catchy slogans.

SPORTS JERSEYS

Speaking of sports—jerseys are in too. Look for one with the logo of your favorite athletic team, whether your sport of choice is baseball, football, or soccer. Or just imitate the baseball look by wearing a white T-shirt with colored sleeves.

Jeans

You probably already have plenty of jeans in your closet. They all count as streetwear fashion! In the early days of streetwear, boys wore their jeans baggy. Some still do, but a more fitted look is popular too, especially for girls. You can wear your jeans as they are. Or if your parents say it's okay, you can add some texture by ripping your jeans with a pair of scissors. You can also fade your jeans by adding a little bleach to the washing machine (with a parent's help).

Shorts

When it comes to shorts, pretty much everything goes. Pick any fabric—cotton, denim, or anything else you like. Wear whatever feels comfortable—from short shorts to longer surfer shorts that reach all the way to your knees.

Dresses

Even though streetwear is casual, dresses are still a big part of the look. They can be loose and flowy, snug and belted, printed, patterned, or solid-colored. As long as they combine style and comfort, they pass muster as streetwear material.

Singer Rita Ova (left) and actress Victoria Justice (right) show off their style with bold printed dresses.

MIX & MATCH

You've got a closet stocked with streetwear must-haves. But that's only the first step. The real trick is to put everything together in a way that works for you. Try mixing and matching styles. Combine streetwear with other items in your wardrobe to create whole new looks! Here are some tips:

- You don't have to go streetwear from head to toe. In most cases, you really need to wear only one piece of streetwear. For example, throw on a snapback hat to add a touch of street flair to a dress.

- Blend dressy and casual looks. Wear a graphic T-shirt with a stylish pair of black or white pants and heels. Or put on a pair of high-top sneakers with a skirt.

Add a bright bag for flair.

- Remember that while streetwear is casual, it's never sloppy. Keep your looks tailored and fitted. Stay in the same color families.

- Don't be afraid to cross gender lines. It's perfectly cool for girls to wear varsity jackets or snapback hats and for guys to wear bling.

Plain shirt + patterned shorts = bold

T-shirt Designs

Don't want to spend your money on someone else's logo T's? Create your own look!

What you need:

- contact paper

- a T-shirt (any color, but your design will show up best on a plain white T-shirt)

- a pair of scissors

- a piece of cardboard

- a sponge

- fabric paint (whatever color you like)

- waxed paper

- iron

What you do:

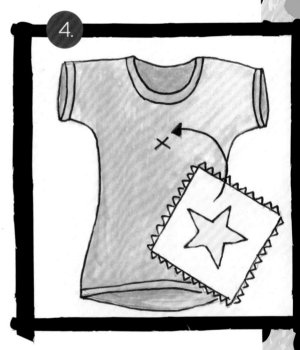

1. Pick out an image or a logo to put on your T-shirt. It can be inspired by any symbol, drawing, or photo that you love.

2. Draw or trace your picture onto a piece of contact paper.

3. Cut out the middle of the design, so you're left with an outline.

4. Peel the backing off the contact paper and stick it to your T-shirt.

5. Put a piece of cardboard between the front and back of your T-shirt so the image doesn't bleed onto the back of the shirt.

6. Dip a sponge into the fabric paint. Press the paint into your design so it fills the whole space.

7. Once you're done painting, peel back the contact paper. Your design should now be on the T-shirt!

8. Let the shirt dry. Then ask an adult to help you iron it over a piece of waxed paper. Time to start thinking of a name for your new T-shirt brand!

DAB ON WITH SPONGE

VOILA!

SHOES

You can't put your best foot forward without a great pair of shoes. Just like with clothes, the magic words are *casual* and *comfortable*. You can still dress up any look, though. Just glitz up your sneaks with studs, or wear heels.

SNEAKERS

Sneakers are the foundation of streetwear. They come in slip-on or lace up, high-top or low-top. Pick the color to match your favorite outfit. Bright colors are in. So are two-toned shoes and wild patterns. Thick or colorful laces add another layer to the look. And of course, don't forget the studs!

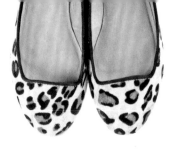

FLATS

These comfy shoes are great for everyday wear. Keep pairs in different colors. Then you can match them up with different outfits!

WEDGES

Wedges have thick soles that make it easy to keep your balance. You can dress them up or down. Worn with a dress, they're a classy, comfortable alternative to heels. With jeans, they can take you anywhere.

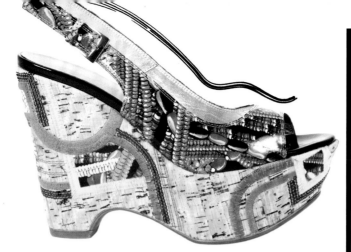

PLATFORMS

These soaring high heels aren't for everyone. First, ask your parents if it's okay for you to wear them. They can be uncomfortable and make walking hard. Save platforms for special occasions.

BOOTS

You don't need massive heels to draw attention to your footwear. Comfortable, durable boots in distinctive colors and all kinds of styles can complete a wide variety of streetwear ensembles.

Studded Sneaks

Turn plain canvas into a swirling, shiny galaxy for the coolest-looking shoes.

What you need:

- a bag of metal studs (or spikes)

- plain sneakers made of soft, thin fabric (such as canvas)

- a small set of pliers

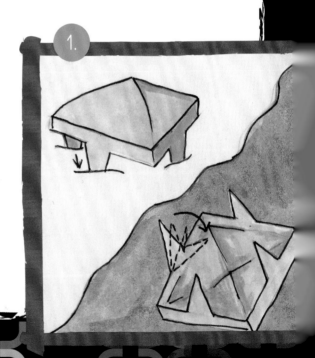

What you do:

1. Poke each stud through the fabric.

2. You'll see two little prongs on the back side of the stud sticking through the fabric of the sneaker. Use your pliers to bend those prongs down. The studs or spikes will then stay in place.

3. Create rows of studs until you've made a design—or covered the whole sneaker!

ACCESSORIES

Streetwear is easy to accessorize. Just throw on a hat, your favorite piece of jewelry, and a scarf. Of course, you don't need these extra touches all the time. On days when you don't want the extra hassle, you can leave your outfit as is.

HATS

You can see snapbacks on the runway.

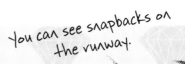

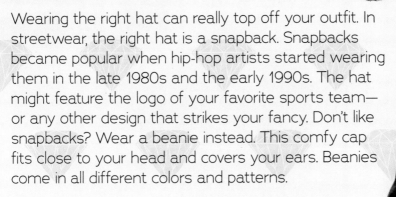

Wearing the right hat can really top off your outfit. In streetwear, the right hat is a snapback. Snapbacks became popular when hip-hop artists started wearing them in the late 1980s and the early 1990s. The hat might feature the logo of your favorite sports team— or any other design that strikes your fancy. Don't like snapbacks? Wear a beanie instead. This comfy cap fits close to your head and covers your ears. Beanies come in all different colors and patterns.

JEWELRY

Streetwear jewelry should be big and bold. It's meant to make a statement. Animal prints, wild colors, and gold accents are all part of the style. Draw some attention with big pendant necklaces or hoop earrings. Bracelets are another way to show off your personal style. You can make your own, using combinations of different-colored beads.

SUNGLASSES

Sunglasses are big—of course! The more bling on them, the cooler they look. You can glitz up a pair of plain sunglasses by gluing rhinestones around the frames.

SCARVES

Big, brightly colored scarves with lively patterns add the perfect accent to your outfit. Even plain scarves in muted colors can be worn with style and flair. You can wear a scarf with anything! Wrap it around your neck in wide, draping loops, or tie it with a loose knot in the front.

OTHER ACCESSORIES

You can add color and bling to your purse, backpack, phone case, or headphones. Just glue on some rhinestones or other gems to create an eye-grabbing accessory.

Beaded Bracelet

Beads are big among fans of street designs. Here's how to make your own beaded bracelets for yourself or your friends.

What you need:

- a pair of scissors

- stretch cord

- beads (any color or type) in a sturdy container

- a large crimp bead

- flat nose pliers

What you do:

1. Cut a piece of cord. Before you make your final snip, measure the cord by wrapping it around your wrist. Don't wrap it too tightly and leave a little extra cord.

2. Put one end of the cord underneath your bead container to hold it down.

3. String the beads onto the cord, one at a time. If you're using beads of different colors, try stringing them in a pattern.

4. Put one end of the cord through the crimp bead.

5. Put the other end of the cord through the crimp bead. Pull it tight.

6. Squeeze your pliers together on the bead to tighten it on the cord.

7. Cut off the extra cord and show off your new wrist-wear!

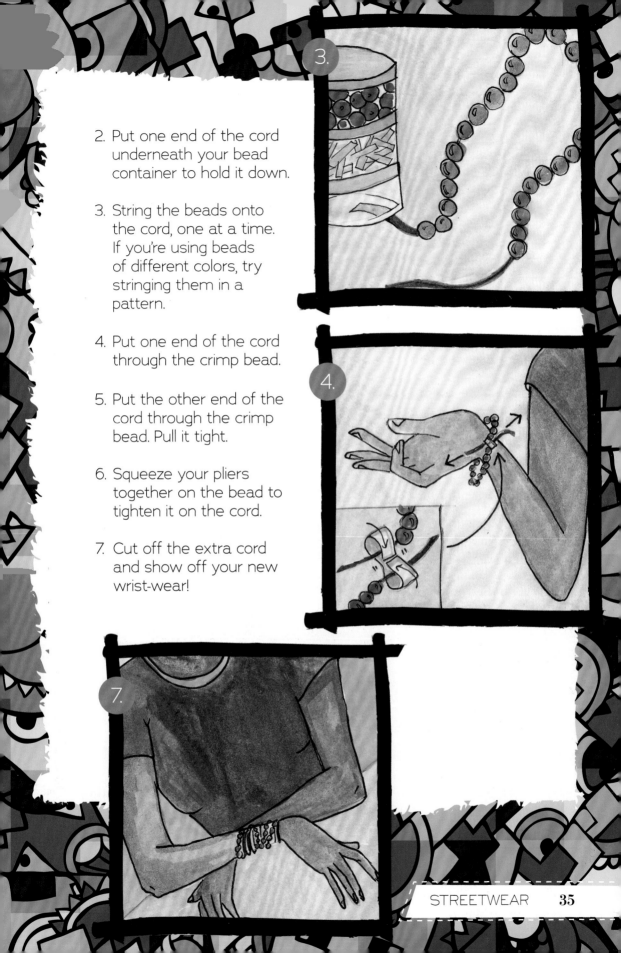

HAIR AND MAKEUP

When it comes to hair and makeup, be yourself! Wear your hair in a tight ponytail, or keep it loose and free. Leave your makeup natural, or—if you have a parent's go-ahead—paint it on boldly. Whatever you like is what's in style.

NATURAL-FLOWING HAIR

Don't want to style your hair in the morning? Wear it loose. Run your hands through your hair to work out the tangles without losing that natural, just-woken-up look. If you've got a bad case of bed head, throw a snapback cap or beanie on top. You can also pull your hoodie up over your head, as long as you're not breaking your school dress code.

Ponytail or Bun

The ponytail is another go-to streetwear style for the long-haired crowd. Keep it loose if you're headed to school or the gym. If you're dressing up, smear on some styling gel and slick it back. Want to go dressier still? Pull your hair up into a bun. To make the bun more distinctive, wear it off to one side of your head.

DIP DYE

Dip-dyed hair is one of the hottest streetwear trends. That's when you dye the tips of your hair bright colors. You can stick with a single shade—say, hot pink—or get a multilayered rainbow effect with several strips of different colors. This style is most often seen on long-haired folks, but anyone can give it a try. Ask your parents before you color your hair! If they say it's okay, have them help you. Better yet, go to a hairstylist to get the color just right.

WILD NAILS

Beiges and muted pinks? Those colors usually don't match most streetwear outfits. Go with something a bit more noticeable, like hot orange or bright yellow. And if you want to be even more unusual, try nail art. You can even create a leopard pattern on your nails.

Adding Color

Bronzers give your skin a sun-kissed look—and are a lot safer than getting an actual tan! Use a big blush brush to sweep the bronzer lightly onto your cheeks.

Going for Bold

For a look that says, "Check me out," start with a bright-colored eye shadow. Purple and blue are good choices. Outline your eyes in dark liner to really make them pop. Finish your makeup with a bright shade of pink or red lipstick.

Stylish Snapback Hat

Want a ready-made look for the mornings when you just feel like hiding your hair? Add some color and style to a plain snapback hat. Who needs a fancy hairdo when the headgear says it all?

What you need:

- fabric glue (or needle and thread)

- patches in your favorite designs

- a plain snapback hat

- fabric markers, felt-tipped pens, or fabric paint

What you do:

1. Glue the patches onto the front and sides of your hat, or ask a parent to help sew them on.

2. Using your markers, pens, or paint, decorate the rest of the hat with your own designs or slogans.

3. Wear your hat backwards over unstyled hair and hit the town. (If your school dress code doesn't allow hats, save this look for weekends or stash your hat in your backpack until class is out.)

Your STREETWEAR Look

Streetwear is all about showing off your creativity. You've got the basics—T-shirts, jeans, sunglasses, and hats. You also have all the info you'll need to put your own special spin on them!

You can create any kind of streetwear look—surfer cool, blinged-out, or something totally new! With streetwear, you're the designer. Mix and match looks and play with styles until you find the one that suits you best. Who knows? You could even become the next big streetwear designer!

Whether it's bright or subtle, streetwear never fails to turn heads.

From the street to the fashion runway, this style is full of surprises.

STREETWEAR RESOURCES

Can't get enough of streetwear? There are plenty of ways to learn more about this style.

Where to Find Streetwear Supplies

- Visit athletic stores, thrift stores, and flea markets for hoodies and sneakers.

- Search surfer stores for shorts and logo T-shirts.

- Look in craft stores and thrift stores for bling and jewelry supplies.

- Check out online auction sites, vintage stores, and thrift shops for vintage sneakers and jewelry.

Where to Find Streetwear Tutorials and Classes

- Find clothing and makeup tutorials on YouTube.

- Take a jewelry-making class to learn how to add bling to your clothes and make your own bracelets and necklaces.

- Look for a T-shirt printing class in your area.

Songs to Spark Your Streetwear Sense

"Ain't Got Time" by M.O.

"Falling" by Haim

"Good Feeling" by Flo Rida

"Happy" by Pharrell Williams

GLOSSARY

bling: flashy, bright-colored, or jeweled accessories

boutique: a small store that sells clothes or accessories

contact paper: paper that is sticky on one side. It can be used for craft projects.

hip-hop: a type of urban youth music and culture

hoodie: a sweatshirt with a hood

icon: someone widely admired for his or her style, smarts, or talent

mogul: a very powerful person

rebel: someone who doesn't follow the rules

snapback: a type of cap with a flat brim

vintage: clothing and jewelry from many years ago

SOURCE NOTES

10. Matt Welty, "Rihanna Shares Why She Mixes Streetwear with High Fashion," *Complex,* March 2, 2013, http://www.complex.com/style/2013/03/rihanna-shares-why-she-mixes-streetwear-with-high-fashion.

11. Woody Hochswender, "SIGNALS; Mean," *New York Times,* June 14, 1992, http://www.nytimes.com/1992/06/14/style/signals-mean.html?pagewanted.

12. Ibid.

14. LinYee Yuan, "X-Pollination of Streetwear," *Theme,* Winter 2007, http://www.thememagazine.com/stories/x-pollination.

15. Ibid.

FURTHER INFORMATION

Girls' Life
http://www.girlslife.com/category/fashion.aspx
Get the scoop on trends, tips, and more in the fashion section of this popular online magazine.

Kids' Fashion
http://kidsfashion.about.com
Find out about the hottest new trends and get tips for styling on a budget.

Sims, Josh. *Cult Streetwear.* **London: Laurence King Publishers, 2010.**
Meet some of the cool, fashion-forward designers who started the whole streetwear style.

Thomas, Isabel. *Being a Fashion Stylist.* **Minneapolis: Lerner Publications, 2013.**
Stylists shape the fashion world. Make sure this awesome job is on your radar.

Vogel, Steven. *Streetwear: The Insider's Guide.* **San Francisco: Chronicle Books, 2007.**
Get an inside look at streetwear fashion from some of the designers who created this look.

Walker, Jackie. *Expressionista: How to Express Your True Self through (and Despite) Fashion.* **New York: Aladdin, 2013.**
This title will help you discover your fashion persona and set up a closet to reflect your sense of style.

INDEX

PHOTO ACKNOWLEDGMENTS

The images in this book are used with the permission of: © Eliks/Shutterstock, p. 3 (letter design); © Che-for-cherry/Shutterstock, p. 3 (bottom); © Paul Vidler/Alamy, p. 5; © Kaponia Aliaksei/Shutterstock, pp. 5 (bottom), 11 (top); © Jeff Kravitz/FilmMagic/Getty Images, p. 6 (bottom left); © DFree/Shutterstock, pp. 6 (bottom right), 7 (top left), 9 (top); © Lev Radi/Shutterstock, pp. 7 (top right), 15 (middle), 17 (top right), 20 (right), 21 (top); © Helga Esteb/Shutterstock, pp. 7 (bottom left), 32 (top right); © Debra L Rothenberg/Getty Images, p. 7 (bottom middle); © Paul A. Hebert/Getty Images, p. 7 (bottom right); © Johnny Nunez/WireImage/Getty Images, p. 8 (top left & top right); © Samir Hussein/WireImage/Getty Images, p. 8 (bottom); © Chelsea Lauren/Getty Images, p. 9 (bottom left); © Ray Tamarra/Getty Images, p. 9 (bottom right); © Neil P. Mockford/FilmMagic/Getty Images, pp. 10 (top and bottom left), 27 (bottom right); © Ollie Millington/WireImage/Getty Images, p. 10 (bottom right); © s_bukley/Shutterstock, pp. 11 (bottom), 31 (top middle), 37 (middle left & middle right), 38 (middle left & middle right); © Khvost/Shutterstock, p. 12 (top left); © iStockphoto/paulprescott72, p. 12 (top middle); © Max2/Bigstock, p. 12 (top right); © Michael Ochs Archives/Getty Images, p. 12 (middle); © Elnur/Bigstock, p. 12 (bottom left); © iStockphoto/yasinguneysu, p. 12 (bottom right); © iStockphoto/UygarGeographic, p. 13 (bottom left); © Igor Borodin/Shutterstock, p. 13 (top); © Cdrin/Shutterstock, p. 13 (bottom right); © Andrea Slatter/Shutterstock, p. 14 (top); © Karkas/Shutterstock, p. 14 (middle left); © Paul Natkin/WireImage/Getty Images, p. 14 (middle right); © Edyta Pawlowska/Shutterstock, p. 15 (top); © Anton Oparin/Shutterstock, pp. 15 (bottom), 18 (top left), 20 (bottom left), 24 (top left & bottom), 27 (top right), 42 (left), 43 (top left); © Piotr Krzeslak/Shutterstock, p. 16 (top left); © R. Gino Santa Maria/Shutterstock, p. 16 (top right); © zhangyang13576997233/Shutterstock, p. 16 (bottom left); © Luna Vandoorne/Shutterstock, pp. 16 (bottom right), 27 (bottom middle); © Dmitri Gromov/Shutterstock, p. 17 (top left); © Can Stock Photo Inc./rmarmion, p. 17 (bottom middle); © Paul Smith/Featureflash/Shutterstock, p. 17 (bottom right); Devone Byrd/PacificCoastNews/Newscom, p. 17 (bottom left); © Prudkov/Shutterstock, p. 18 (top right); © Samuel Borges Photography/Shutterstock, p. 18 (bottom left); © mimagephotography/Shutterstock, p. 18 (bottom right); © Elnur/Shutterstock, p. 19 (top left); © Alexandra Glen/Featureflash/Shutterstock, pp. 19 (top right), 43 (bottom left); © Simon Burchell/Featureflash/Shutterstock, p. 19 (bottom left); © Jaguar PS/Shutterstock, pp. 19 (bottom right), 21 (bottom left); © catwalker/Shutterstock, pp. 21 (bottom right), 31 (top right), 43 (top right); © Jason Merritt/Getty Images, p. 24 (top right); © iStockphoto/AlenaPaulus, p. 24 (middle); © Africa Studio/Shutterstock, pp. 25 (right), 38 (middle bottom); © WilleeCole/Shutterstock, p. 25 (left); © PhotoNAN/Shutterstock, p. 26 (top left); © Vankad/Bigstock, p. 26 (top middle); © iStockphoto/Chiyacat, p. 26 (top right); © Gromovataya/Shutterstock, p. 26 (middle left); © Guzel Studio/Shutterstock, pp. 26 (middle right & bottom left), 33 (middle left); © inchic/Shutterstock, p. 26 (bottom right); © William Perugini/Shutterstock, p. 26 (bottom left); © Palych/Bigstock, p. 27 (top left); © Ruslan Kudrin/Shutterstock, p. 30 (top); © Polryaz/Shutterstock, p. 30 (middle top right); © Photosync/Shutterstock, p. 30 (middle top left); © Aaron Amat/Shutterstock, p. 30 (middle bottom); © Marek R. Swadzba/Shutterstock, p. 30 (bottom left); © Suzi Nelson/Shutterstock, p. 30 (bottom right); © Sweet November studio/Shutterstock, p. 31 (top left); © David Acosta Allely/Shutterstock, p. 31 (bottom left); © Cosma/Bigstock, p. 31 (bottom right); © Featureflash/Shutterstock, pp. 32 (top left & middle), 38 (top); © K2 images/Shutterstock, p. 32 (bottom left); © Karkas/Bigstock, p. 32 (bottom middle); © Andreas Gradin/Shutterstock, p. 32 (bottom right); © michaeljung/Shutterstock, p. 33 (top left); © Wacpan/Bigstock, p. 33 (top right); © JanVlcek/Shutterstock, p. 33 (middle right); © hifashion/Shutterstock, p. 33 (bottom); © Nixx Photography/Shutterstock, p. 36 (top); © Ardni/Shutterstock, p. 36 (bottom right); © iordani/Bigstock, p. 36 (middle), 39 (middle); © Samuel Borges/Bigstock, p. 36 (bottom left); © iStockphoto/iconogenic, p. 37 (top); © Luminaimages/Shutterstock, p. 37 (bottom); © Alexandra Lande/Shutterstock, p. 38 (bottom); © Gvictoria/Dreamstime, p. 39 (top); © Yastremska/Bigstock, p. 39 (top left); © Olga Ekaterincheva/Shutterstock, p. 39 (bottom left); © Tukkata/Shutterstock, p. 39 (bottom right); © Miro Vrlik Photography/Shutterstock, p. 42 (right); © Kirstin Sinclair/FilmMagic/Getty Images, p. 43 (bottom right).

Backgrounds: © Dmitrii Vlasov/Shutterstock, pp. 1, 11, 34–35; © UyUy/Shutterstock, p. 2; © Wacomka/Shutterstock, pp. 4–5; © Tukkki/Shutterstock, pp. 6–7, 8, 9, 10, 22–23, 44–45, 46–47, 48; © Yuyi/Shutterstock, p. 13; © Picsfive/Shutterstock, p. 14; © Vector Ninja/Shutterstock, pp. 15, 17; © run4it/Bigstock, pp. 20–21; © Gudinny/Shutterstock, p. 28–29, 40–41, 43–44; © IrenD/Shutterstock, p. 31. © Andrey_Kuzmin/Shutterstock, p. 33.

Front cover: © Dmitrii Vlasov/Shutterstock (green background & colorful background); © Photosync/Shutterstock (earrings); © Polryaz/Shutterstock (watch); © iStockphoto/Rouzes (sunglasses); © Palych/Bigstock (shoes); © iStockphoto/Jitalia17 (jeans); © Karkas/Bigstock (scarf); © zhangyang13576997233/Shutterstock (sweater); © Adisa/Shutterstock (sneakers); © Marek R. Swadzba/Shutterstock (bracelets).

Back cover: © UyUy/Shutterstock (leopard pattern); © Suzi Nelson/Shutterstock (purse); © iStockphoto/yasinguneysu (sneakers).